A Child's Introduction to Understanding PANDAS

Elizabeth Gibbs

A Child's Introduction to Understanding PANDAS
written by Elizabeth Gibbs
photographs by Elizabeth Gibbs

Information about PANDAS was referenced from:

"PANDAS: Frequently Asked Questions about Pediatric Autoimmune Neuropsychiatric Disorders Associated with Streptococcal Infections." NIMH National Institute of Mental Health. N.p., 18 Oct. 2012. Web. 6 Dec. 2012. <http://www.nimh.nih.gov/health/publications/pandas/pandas-frequently-asked-questions-about-pediatric-autoimmune-neuropsychiatric-disorders-associated-with-streptococcal-infections.shtml>

PANDAS Network. N.p., n.d. Web. 6 Dec. 2012. <http://pandasnetwork.org/>

"Pandas Resource Network." Pandas Resource Network. N.p., n.d. Web. 6 Dec. 2012. <http://www.pandasresourcenetwork.org/>

Personal conversations between the author and her daughter's pediatrician.

All other material was developed from the personal experiences
of the author and is not intended to be used as medical advice.

ISBN: 978-1480153707
ISBN-13: 1480153702
elizabethgibbs-author.blogspot.com

This book is dedicated to my
family for their ongoing
love and support.

Do you know one of the things that makes me so special?

I'm Dora Grace, and I have **PANDAS.**

No silly! Not like a panda <u>bear</u>!

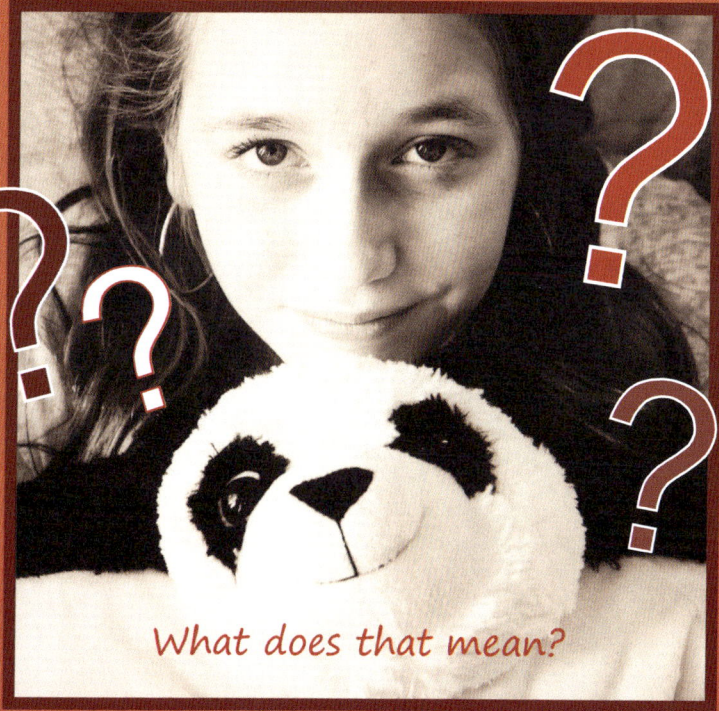

What does that mean?

The kind of *PANDAS* I have is very special and unique. Since you are reading this you probably either have *PANDAS* yourself or know someone who does. The first step to supporting someone with *PANDAS* is to better understand it.

Let's start by finding out exactly what **PANDAS** is...

Pediatric
This means it is something only children get.

Autoimmune
This is when your body fights itself

in the same way it fights germs.

Neuropsychiatric
This is a big word to say when your body is sick and

makes your mind (thoughts and behaviors) sick too.

Disorders

This is when something is not working quite right.

Associated with

This means connected or related to.

Streptococci

This is the doctor name for the germ that causes strep infections - most of us know it as strep throat.

So what do all of these words put together mean?

When a child with **PANDAS** gets a strep infection the part of their body that fights germs - the immune system - gets confused. It thinks that a part of the brain is really the strep germs and tries to fight that instead. This not only makes the brain upset, causing the child to behave differently, but the body gets so distracted it forgets to fight the real strep, making it very hard to get better.

7

Children who find out they have *PANDAS* may first
go to their doctor for help with some new behaviors.
Most of the new behaviors are started because of
worries the child has probably never had before.

There are two groups of these behaviors that
children with *PANDAS* can have - *OCD* or *TICS*
(and some have both).

OCD, or *Obsessive Compulsive Disorder*, is when
you worry about something and your mind tells you to do
things to help get rid of the worry.   Some of these worries
that a lot of children with *PANDAS* have are...

8

Fear of Germs - Their mind may tell them
to wash their hands over and over again.

Checking, Counting, and Repeating - Their mind may
tell them that something bad will happen if they do not go back
and double check, count things, or do something over and over.

Order and Lines - Their mind may tell them that something
does not look right and that they need to move it or fix it.

Now, what about the second type of new behavior?

TICS, or Motor TICS...

This is when your body makes quick movements that you do not want it to. Some of these movements are...

eye blinking or squinting

nose twitching

shrugging shoulders

moving head quickly

Here are some vocal – or spoken – tics:

coughing or throat clearing

repeating sounds or words

saying mean words without wanting to

There are many other things that can come along with

PANDAS...

BEDTIME WORRIES

Sad for no reason

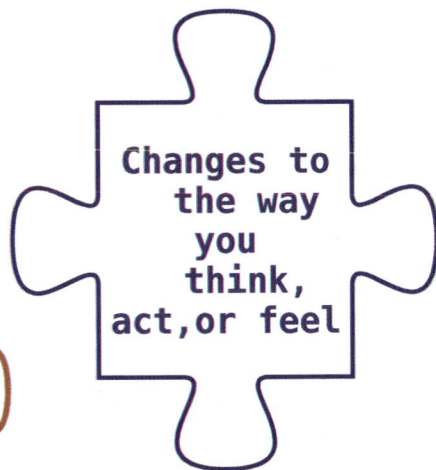

Changes to the way you think, act, or feel

Afraid to be away from parents

REALLY Angry

EXTRA SENSITIVE TO TOUCH AND SOUND

Grumpy for no reason

Crying Spells

Wanting to hit or kick

Find it hard to pay attention

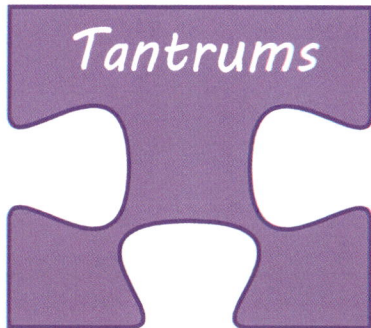
Tantrums

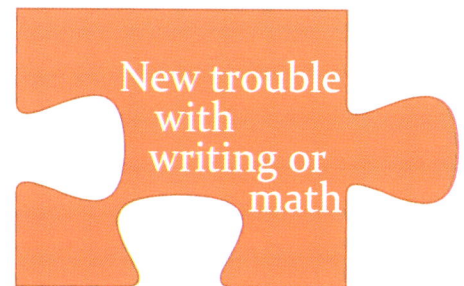
New trouble with writing or math

Do you know what the hardest part of having *PANDAS* is for me?

Knowing

what

to do

with all

of these

thoughts

and

feelings.

That is why

my parents and I

came up with a new

PANDAS...

Plan

Ahead

Needs

Doctor

Appointments

Stress relief

17

Plan Ahead

Since a lot of the things that come with **PANDAS**
come and go with the strep infections,
it is a good idea to make a *plan* while the
infection is gone and you are feeling your best.
That way when you get strep again,
and all of those worries and feelings
start to show up, you will be ready.

Some familes even have a code word the **PANDAS**
child can say as a way of letting their parents
know that the feelings are starting to come back.

Our parents will not know how we feel unless we tell them!

Are you going to have a code word?

Do you have brothers or sisters that need help understanding PANDAS?

What about your best friends?

Do they know why you get

so upset sometimes?

What are some things that can be done now that will help the next time you get an infection?

Needs

What you *need* from your parents is something else that is very important to share as you *plan ahead* together. Everyone is different when they get upset, and if someone does not know what you *need* they will probably give you what they *think* you want.   Like my Mom, she *needs* hugs and kisses when she is upset, but me - I like to be left alone! So when she tries to give me hugs it makes me even more upset.

Also, it is a good idea to make sure all members of your household understand your *needs* so they are comfortable and know what to do when you are upset.   My parents and I even decided to speak with my teacher about my *needs* while I am at school.

Do you need to talk about it now?

How about a hug?

Do you want to be left alone?

Do you feel like going to your room where it is quiet?

KEEP OUT!

I tape this to my door when I want to be left alone!

Doctor Appointments

This used to be the hardest part of having **PANDAS** for me.   I never liked to go to the *doctor*. That was until I started listening to her and telling her more about me.   Soon after that, and when I began to do the things she asked me to try, I started to feel better and could see that she really does care about me!

I am very lucky to have a *doctor* that already knows about **PANDAS**.

I know that some children may see many *doctors* before they find one that really understands.

What do you like about seeing your doctor?

Have you tried talking to your doctor about how you are feeling?

Are you afraid?
If yes, what are you afraid of?

Do you have any questions for your doctor when you see them next?

If yes, it is a good idea to write them down now, so you will remember.

I asked my doctor if I could try swallowing pills next time – and she said yes!

Stress relief

Figuring out what helps you to relieve *stress*
will help when you have an infection and find yourself
filled with sadness or anger.   So many times we do not
know how to get rid of the anger so we end up yelling at
or trying to hit or kick our parents or other people we love.

There are much better ways to help yourself feel better,
so it is important to add this to your *plan* and know
what you are going to do when the anger comes back.

Some children feel better when they do something
active where others *need* to do something quiet.

31

Bounce a Ball...

This is one of
my favorites!

Dance - Turn on some music
and move all around your room!

Jump - with a jump rope,
mini trampolene, or hopscotch

Those that need

to do something

active can try...

Go for a walk with a parent

Those that need something quiet can try....

Journal - Write out all of the mad or hurtful words inside of you. This way you can still get it out without accidentally hurting someone else's feelings.

Listen to music - Have some soft music set aside just for these times.

Read - This is one of my Mom's favorites. She says it is a way to escape the stress and visit someone else's world for awhile, giving your mind and body time to relax.

Practice Yoga

33

Have you come up with any ideas
or thoughts for your own **plan** yet?

Maybe your parents, friends,

or brothers and sisters will

have some suggestions to share.

Use the following pages to write down
your ideas, along with your answers to the
questions you read earlier in this book.

Be sure to include all the parts of your *plan*, what you *need* from your friends and family, and information about your *doctor appointments*.

Also, there are pages for you to write down ideas of what you are going to try the next time you get angry or *stressed*.   Make notes of things you have tried - what helped and what didn't.

Needs

Made in the USA
Lexington, KY
26 October 2014